READY, SET, DRAW!

DINOSAURS AND OTHER PREHISTORIC CREATURES YOU CAN DRAW

Nicole Brecke

Patricia M Stockland

Lerner Books • London • New York • Minneapolis

The images in this book are used with the permission of: © iStockphoto.com/Dzianis Miraniuk, p. 4;
© iStockphoto.com, pp. 4, 5, 9, 31; © iStockphoto.com/Boris Yankov, p. 5; © iStockphoto.com/JR
Trice, p. 5; © iStockphoto.com/George Olsson, p. 7; © iStockphoto.com/Alberto L. Pomares G., p. 11;
© iStockphoto.com/Andriy Myahkov, p. 15; © iStockphoto.com/Phil Morley, p. 19; © iStockphoto.com/
Sebastien Cote, p. 23; © iStockphoto.com/Les Cunliffe, p. 27.

Front cover: © iStockphoto.com/Sebastien Cote (coast); © iStockphoto.com/George Olsson (forest);
© Iofoto/Dreamstime.com (hand).

The publisher wishes to thank Thomas R. Holtz Jr., Senior Lecturer in Vertebrate Paleontology,
University of Maryland, College Park, for serving as a consultant on this title.

Edited by Mari Kesselring
Research by Emily Temple

First published in the United Kingdom in 2011 by
Lerner Books,
Dalton House,
60 Windsor Avenue,
London SW19 2RR

Website address: www.lernerbooks.co.uk

British Library Cataloguing in Publication Data

Brecke, Nicole.
Dinosaurs and other prehistoric creatures you can draw.–
(Ready, set, draw!)
1. Dinosaurs in art – Juvenile literature. 2. Drawing –
Technique – Juvenile literature.
I. Title II. Series
743.6-dc22

ISBN-13: 978 0 7613 6886 1

Printed in China
First published in the United States of America in 2010

TABLE OF CONTENTS

ABOUT THIS BOOK

SuperCrocs, *Triceratops* and *Tyrannosaurus rex*! Be on the lookout for these ancient beasts. With the help of this book, you can begin drawing your own prehistoric pal. Soon you'll know how to create many different dinosaurs and reptiles.

Follow these steps to create each animal. Each drawing begins with a basic form. The form is made up of a line and a shape or two. These lines and shapes will help you make your drawing the correct size.

A First, read all the steps and look at the pictures. Then use a pencil to lightly draw the line and shapes shown in RED. You will erase these lines later.

B Next, draw the lines shown in BLUE.

C Keep going! Once you have completed a step, the colour of the line changes to BLACK. Follow the BLUE line until you're done.

WHAT YOU WILL NEED

PENCIL SHARPENER

COLOURED PENCILS

HELPFUL HINTS

Be creative. Use your imagination. Read about *Ankylosaurus*, *Apatosaurus* and *Stegosaurus*. Then follow the steps to sketch your own dynamic dino.

Practise drawing different lines and shapes. All of your drawings will start with these.

Use very light pencil lines when you are drawing.

RUBBER

Helpful tips and hints will offer you good ideas on making the most of your sketch.

PENCIL

Colours are exciting. Try to use a variety of shades. This will add value, or depth, to your finished drawings.

PAPER

Keep practising, and have fun!

HOW TO DRAW
APATOSAURUS

This massive dinosaur was one of the biggest plant eaters to ever roam Earth. With a long neck, a long tail and a big, big body. It was previously known as *Brontosaurus*. *Apatosaurus* had to spend most of its time eating just to grow and stay strong. Some scientists think the animal ate more than 454 kilograms (1,000 pounds) of food each day. *Apatosaurus* lived in heavily forested areas. It munched on ferns (both giant and small), shrubs and treetops. But other dinosaurs sometimes attacked and ate *Apatosaurus*.

1 Lightly draw a big base circle and a small base circle. Connect them with a long curving baseline.

2 Draw a jaw, a mouth, a nose and a head around the small base circle. Make a long neck line. Add another curving line for the rest of the neck and the back.

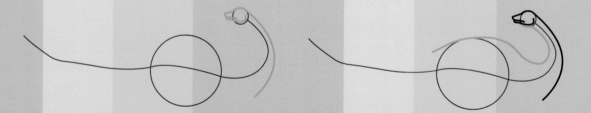

3

Make two long lines that join in a loop to form the tail.

4

Use four bumpy vertical lines and two short horizontal lines to make the legs. Add a belly line. Draw the other legs and feet.

5

Carefully erase your baseline and shapes. Add two nostrils and an eye.

6

Now it's time to colour your *Apatosaurus*!

HOW TO DRAW
TRICERATOPS

The tank like *Triceratops* looked fierce. The three horns on its large, frilled head were a good defence against predators. Its mouth was shaped like a parrot's beak. This shape helped the big herbivore, or plant-eater, tear leaves and branches off trees and cycads, one of its favourite palm like foods. *Triceratops* travelled in herds, similar to modern-day elephants. Sticking with a group helped *Triceratops* protect itself. Together, the animals were even better than a lone *Triceratops* at fending off the hungry *Tyrannosaurus rex*. *Triceratops* laid its eggs in a nest on the ground.

1 Draw two base ovals and a curving baseline. On the smaller oval, make two large horns, a small spike and a hooked mouth and a jaw.

2 Add a frilled C shape to the back of the head. Draw a bumpy neckline. Make a large curved back and a thick pointed tail.

3

Use two longer curving lines for the back leg. Add a short line and toes. Make a shorter front leg, a short line and toes. Draw a belly line. Add the other two legs and feet.

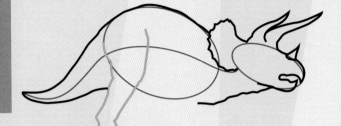

4 Carefully erase your base shapes and baseline. Draw small curves along the frilled edge. Add an eye, an eyebrow and a nostril.

5 Now it's time to colour your *Triceratops*!

HOW TO DRAW SUPERCROC

Sarcosuchus imperator—or SuperCroc—ruled the Sahara region of Africa more than 100 million years ago, when the area was a swamp. This giant crocodile relative used its 132 supersharp teeth to hunt and kill prey. SuperCroc was a super hunter. And it was supersized. The animal likely grew to 12 metres (40 feet) in length. Scientists think an adult SuperCroc weighed 8,165 kilograms (18,000 pounds). The SuperCroc had protective bony plates on its back, which acted like a shield. Dinosaurs probably didn't bother SuperCroc.

1

Draw a small base oval and a long C-shaped baseline. Add a forehead and a long snout to the base oval. Make a skinny V shape. Add a short jaw line. Draw a bumpy neck line.

2

Make a bumpy back line. Connect two curved lines for the tail. Use an L shape for the back leg. Add a curved line and claws. Use a C shape for the front leg. Add a curved line and claws. Draw a belly line.

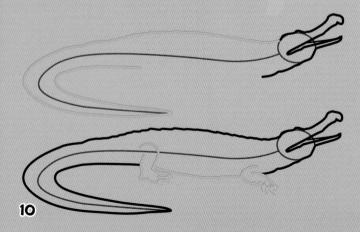

3

Start at the head and draw another bumpy, curving line down the back to the curve in the tail. Carefully erase your baseline and base shape.

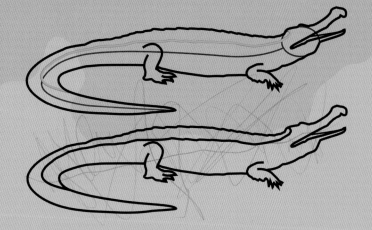

4

Draw about seventeen short lines between the two lines along the back. Draw short spikes down each side of the tail. Add an eye and sharp teeth.

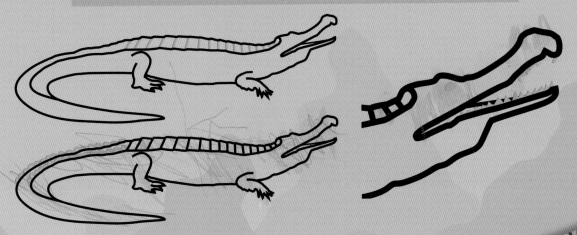

5

Now it's time to colour your SuperCroc!

HOW TO DRAW
ICHTHYOSAURUS

From 200 million to 190 million years ago, *Ichthyosaurus* swam in a giant, ancient sea. These water reptiles were similar to modern dolphins. *Ichthyosaurus* had nostrils and lungs, and it had to rise to the water's surface to breathe. The large 'fish lizards' hunted for shrimp, squid like creatures called belemnites, and other marine prey. Its sharp teeth, long snout and jaw and keen eyesight made it a very good hunter. *Ichthyosaurus* had a dorsal fin like a dolphin's, but its tail fin was vertical like a fish's. This type of fin helped *Ichthyosaurus* move quickly through the water.

1 Draw a base circle and base oval that touch. Make a curving baseline through the centre. Add a long V shape to the top. Draw a long jaw line and a short neck line.

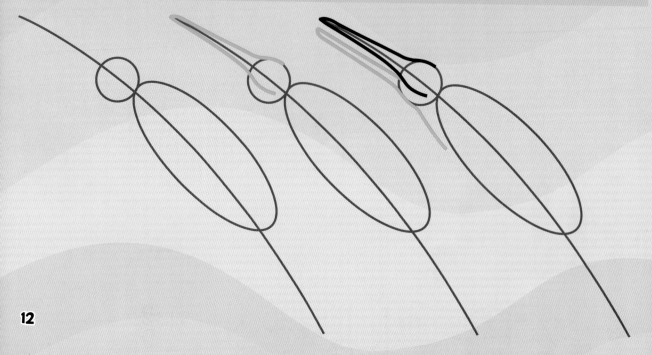

2 Add a curved line for the back and a pointed dorsal fin. Use two bent lines for the tail, and connect them with a curved line.

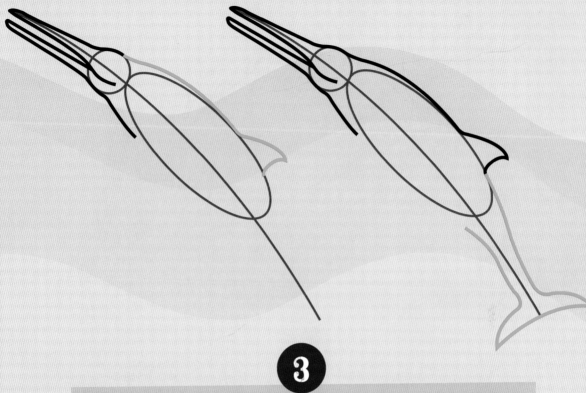

3 Draw a bent U shape for the front flipper and a smaller bent U for the back flipper. Make a belly line. Add the other flippers.

4 Carefully erase your base shapes and baseline. Add two circles for the eye. Draw two rows of teeth.

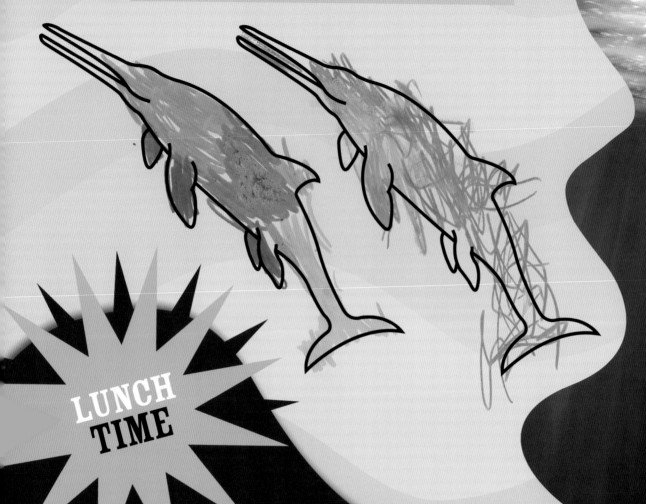

LUNCH TIME

Bones and shells have been found in *Ichthyosaurus*'s fossilized stomach and vomit remains.

DRAW A BELEMNITE!

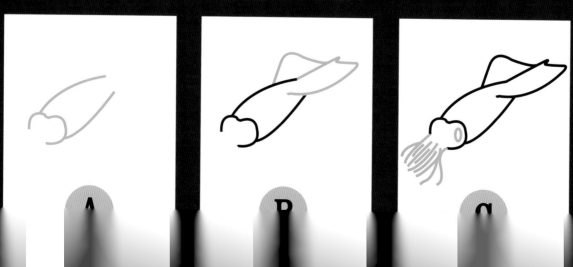

A

B

C

Ichthyosaurus
was about
2 metres
(7 feet)
long.

5

Now it's time
to colour your
Ichthyosaurus!

SCIENTISTS think *Ichthyosaurus*'s large
eyes helped it find prey underwater.

HOW TO DRAW
TYRANNOSAURUS REX

Who is one of the biggest meat-eaters you know? If you lived 68 to 65 million years ago, the answer might be *Tyrannosaurus rex*. This massive carnivore could bite off and swallow 45 kilograms (100 pounds) in a single chomp. More than sixty banana-sized teeth helped the dinosaur tear through its prey. Scientists also think that *T. rex* scavenged for carrion. This means *T. rex* would eat dead, decaying animals that it found. A large tail and strong back legs helped *T. rex* balance its giant head.

1

Draw a base circle and a base oval. Connect them with a long baseline.

2

Make a large head, a snout and a jaw following the base oval.

3 Draw a curved neck line and a bumpy back. Follow the baseline to add a long, large pointed tail.

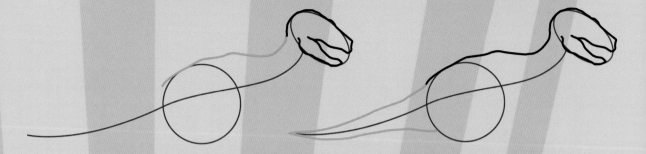

4 Use two long, bumpy vertical lines to make the back leg. Add large toes. Make a pointed claw on each. Using shorter lines, draw the other back leg. Add toes and claws.

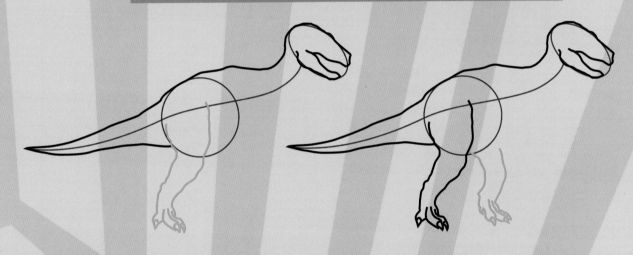

5 Draw a slightly dented belly line. Use an S shape to make a forearm and claws. Add a curved line for the neck. Draw the other forearm and claws.

6 Before finishing the face, carefully erase your base shapes and baseline.

7 Draw a small oval for the eye. Add a bent line above the eye. Draw a nostril. Add a curved line above it. Fill the mouth with large teeth using V shapes.

Did you know...

FROM THE TIP OF ITS NOSE TO THE TIP OF ITS TAIL, *T. REX* WAS NEARLY 12 METRES (40 FEET) LONG.

The word *Tyrannosaurus* means 'tyrant lizard.'

8 Now it's time to colour your *Tyrannosaurus rex*!

HOW TO DRAW PTERODACTYLUS

The name *Pterodactylus* means wing finger.
Its wings were similar to bat wings. Tip to tip, its wings
could stretch up to 2.4 metres (8 feet). *Pterodactylus* had a
beak full of needle like teeth. It wasn't a dinosaur or a bird.
It was a type of pterosaur, or flying reptile. This predator
ate fish. Scientists believe it would have scooped up fish,
similar to what a pelican does. *Pterodactylus* could hold
many fish in a pouch inside its throat. Hollow bones helped
the reptile fly by making it very light. *Pterodactylus* had
sharp claws, a short tail and fur.

1

Draw a wide, bent baseline.
Add a small base circle. Make
a long W shape for the beak.

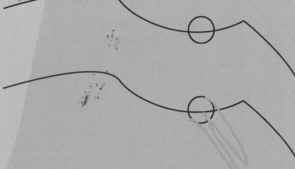

2

Draw three short,
straight lines behind
the head. Add a bumpy
spike shape. Add another
bumpy line along the top
of the spike.

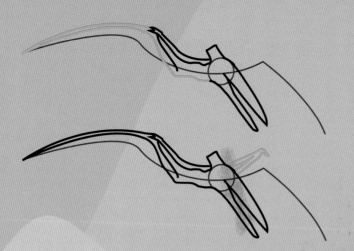

3 Use two connected curving lines to make the top of the wing. Add a slightly dented line. Draw a V with a crooked tip. Add a small V inside this.

4 Draw a large V shape and a short line to finish the other wing. Finish the first wing. Draw a curved line.

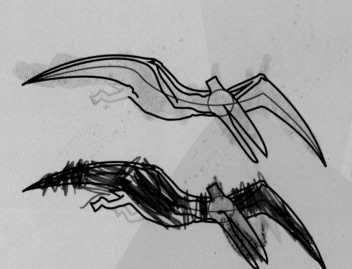

5 Draw a leg and a small, pointed tail. Add the other leg.

Fast Fact...
PTERODACTYLUS LIVED DURING THE JURASSIC PERIOD, MORE THAN 150 MILLION YEARS AGO.

6 Carefully erase your base shape and baseline.

7

Draw an eye using an oval, a short curved line, and a centre dot. Use a long thin triangle for the nostril. Add sharp teeth and a line on the beak.

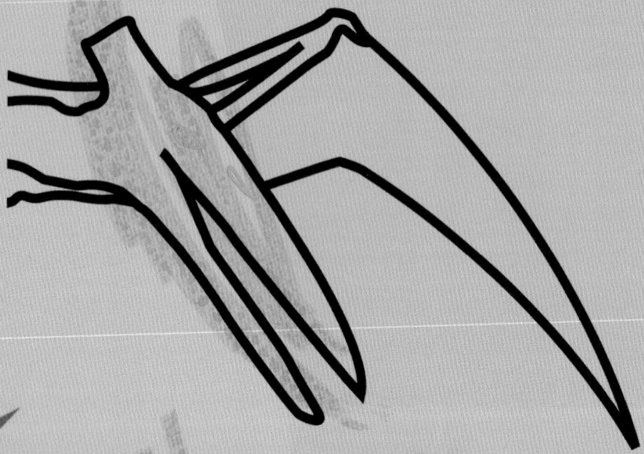

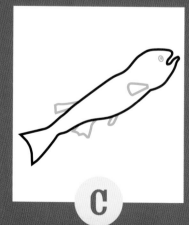

DINNER DELIGHT

Like many modern birds, *Pterodactylus* fed on a variety of fish.

DRAW A FISH!

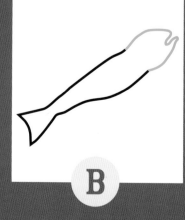

A

B

C

8 Now it's time to colour your *Pterodactylus*!

TRY THIS
Use bright colours for *Pterodactylus*'s crest.

HOW TO DRAW
STEGOSAURUS

Stegosaurus **is known for the many plates that ran down its back.** With spikes on the end of its long tail, this dinosaur looked tough. All of this armour made *Stegosaurus* look bigger than it actually was. The plates along its back were not attached to the skeleton. Instead, the thin bony structures were part of the dinosaur's skin. The dinosaur used these spikes to protect itself. These plates might have helped *Stegosaurus* cool down or stay warm too. This plant-eater's main weapon was its tail. The large *Stegosaurus* would whip the spiky end toward its predators.

1

Draw a large base oval and a small base oval. Add a long, humped baseline. Make a bumpy sideways V shape on the smaller oval.

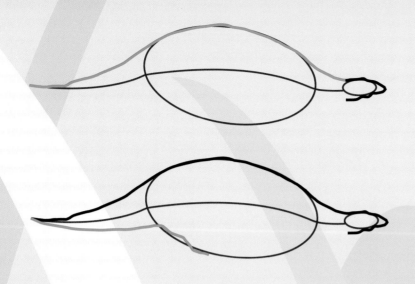

2

Draw a long, bumpy curved line for the neck, the back and the top of the tail. Add the bottom of the tail. Make a shorter dented line.

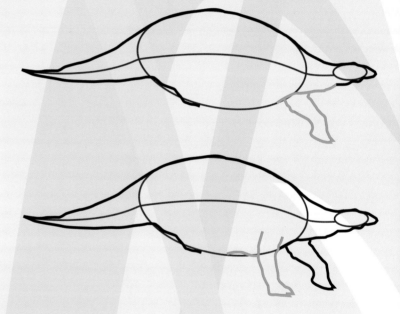

Add a rough line for the front of the neck. Make the first leg and the foot. Add the second leg and the foot and a short line.

3

4

Draw the back legs using longer lines. Add a small line to the front of each foot.

5

Use four angled lines to draw each of the plates along the back.

6

Draw a second row of plates using V shapes above the first row. Add angled lines.

7

Carefully erase your baseline and base shapes.

8

Add two pairs of spikes to the end of the tail. Draw a small eye and a line for the mouth.

Stegosaurus lived about 150 million years ago.

HELPFUL HINT
Colour with browns and tans to give the plates texture.

9

Now it's time to colour your *Stegosaurus*!

HOW TO DRAW ANKYLOSAURUS

Berries, leaves and other plant parts made perfect meals for *Ankylosaurus.* This wide-bodied plant-eater had very small teeth. Although it didn't eat meat, *Ankylosaurus* had to protect itself from becoming dinner for other dinosaurs such as *T. rex. Ankylosaurus* was built like a living tank. Hard, flat, bony plates lined its body. Spikes grew above its eyes. The dinosaur also had a heavy clubbed tail it could bash into enemies. *Ankylosaurus* may have even had colouring that helped it blend into its leafy surroundings.

1 Draw a large base oval and a small base oval. Make a long, curving baseline. Add a rounded U shape for the head and the neck. Make a small line for the mouth.

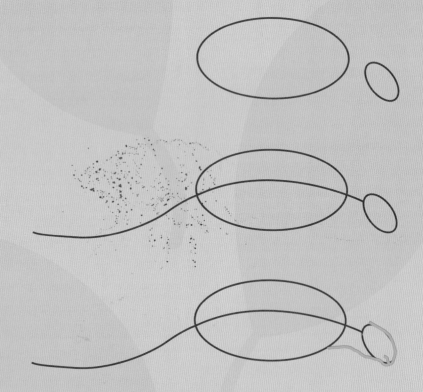

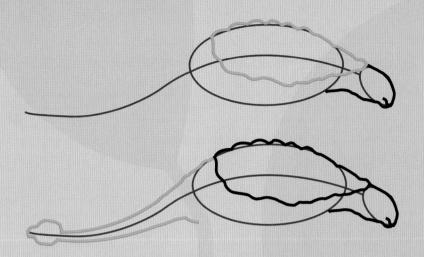

Make a large, bumpy pointed oval behind the head. Draw a lumped, open oval at the far left tip of the baseline. Use two long, curved lines to finish the tail.

3

Draw slightly bent vertical lines for the back leg and the front leg. Finish each leg by creating a foot with short, pointy lines. Draw the belly line. Draw the second back leg. Add the other front leg using curved lines.

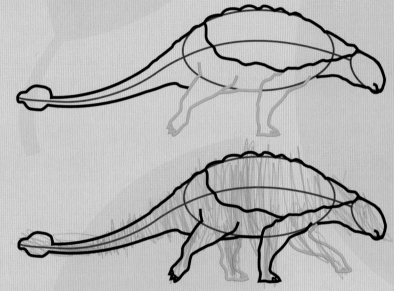

4

Carefully erase your baseline and base shapes. Add eight wavy vertical lines to the back.

5

Then draw three wavy horizontal lines across the back. Add a long line down the tail. Make short curved lines across the top of the tail. Draw an eye and a spike above it.

HATCH A BATCH

Each baby *Ankylosaurus* hatched from an egg, which was guarded by its mother.

DRAW A NEST AND EGGS!

A

B

C

ANKYLOSAURUS lived about 68 to 65 million years ago. It was probably one of the last dinosaurs to exist on Earth.

TRY THIS
Use shading to create depth.

6 Now it's time to colour your *Ankylosaurus*!

FURTHER READING

Benton, Michael. *The Best Ever Book of Dinosaurs*. London: Kingfisher Books Ltd, 2001.

The Big Book of Dinosaurs. London: Dorling Kindersley, 1994.

Bingham, Caroline. *Dinosaur Encyclopedia*. London: Dorling Kindersley, 2009.

DinosaurFacts
http://www.dinosaurfacts.org/

The Dinosaur Society
http://www.dinosaursociety.com/kids-gallery.php

Natural History Museum
http://www.nhm.ac.uk/kids-only/dinosaurs/

Ross, Kathy. *Crafts for Kids Who Are Learning about Dinosaurs*. Minneapolis: Millbrook Press, 2008.

Turnbull, Stephanie. *Dinosaurs*. London: Usborne Publishing Ltd, 2006.

INDEX